This work is dedicated to unwavering commitment and passion of all my students and interns of Faculty of Occupational Therapy, JSSAHER for believing in me and for their constant support throughout the process.

BASICS OF MANAGERIAL SKILLS FOR THERAPIST AND MEDICAL PROFESSIONALS

MANAGERIAL SKILLS FOR ENTREPRENEUR AND THERAPIST

DR AMITABH KISHOR DWIVEDI

Made with ♥ on the Notion Press Platform
www.notionpress.com

Contents

Preface

The Need for having a simple, straightforward but effective book that will guide young individuals to how to pave their path soon after their graduation or post-graduation, was immense. This book was purely written in intension to give support and guidance to the upcoming Occupational therapists and other medical professionals, so that they could understand how they could put up their own startup and also understand the dynamics of the industry.

This book is basically divided in 5 whole chapters along with their subtopics using most simple language. The approach is very practical with charts, tables, examples etc...

In more than 20 years of my work experience, in which 9 years I have worked as professor and Dean, I have seen many young individual's quandary when they want to start their career. It is very obvious that they may face various challenges and hurdles despite their proficiency in both practical and theoretical knowledge. Because in actual setup there lies a huge gap between theory and the clinical practical aspects. Here, I remember the saying of Swami Vivekananda that "Aaj *ka education system Hanuman kood ki tarah hai"*. Meaning which he wants to convey is that our education system when enter in a job market or in process of seeking job, the exceptional skills and knowledge acquired during graduation might not be sufficient. Many may have a sound knowledge but that might not be sufficient. When coming to job market the skills alone will not help the individual to deliver their best. That's why jumping from graduation to job market depicts Hanuman kood that is illustrated in "Ramayana" where it was shown in search of Sita, Lord Hanuman jumped and crossed the sea which was nearly impossible. Likewise, many graduates tend to portray Hanuman kood but eventually fail since they fail to understand not only" skills" but also the path and ways used to imply these exceptional skills are also necessary.

By this book, I aim to initiate the process of narrow down the gap mentioned above. Thus, I intended the publication of this book.

I also acknowledge and show my gratitude towards each one who had been putting their constant and sustained efforts to turn the vision of this book into a concrete manifestation.

Acknowledgements

I acknowledge and show my gratitude towards each one who had been putting their constant and sustained efforts to turn the vision of this book into a concrete manifestation. I also acknowledge the efforts of contributors for their valuable input to this book.

CONTRIBUTERS

Alvina Ann Chacko - Intern of batch 2022-23, Faculty of Occupational Therapy Department, JSS Academy of Higher Education and Research, Mysore. She played an integral role in shaping the foundation of this book through their diligent work on the initial draft. Her insightful contributions and dedications laid the groundwork for the book. She established the framework authored content on various topics. Her sustained and remarkable efforts made this book achievable.

Donna K Iype and Abiya Binoy – Interns of batch 2023- 24, Faculty of Occupational Therapy Department, JSS Academy of Higher Education and Research, Mysore. Their key contribution was in carefully editing and polishing the manuscript so as to bring forth the refined and cohesive narrative. Additionally, demonstrated in adding new topics thus enriching the overall content of the book. Their dedication to precision and comprehensive understanding significantly enhanced the early steps of publications.

Prologue

Managerial skills play a crucial role of therapists and medical professionals as they contribute to effective leadership, communication, and decision making within health care settings.

A book focussing on managerial skills can provide insight to understand how to lead and motivate teams in an health care environment, ensuring effective patient care and collaboration. Enhancement of communication skills which involve interacting with colleagues, patients and other healthcare professionals. Developing the ability to make informed decisions that make impact patient care, resource allocation, and overall, health care service delivery. To efficiently manage time and resources, equipping medical professionals with problem-solving techniques, exploring ethical dilemmas and decision – making in context of health care and fostering teamwork and collaboration among medical professionals, promoting a positive work environment.

This book can be a valuable resource for both aspiring and practicing therapists and medical professionals, helping them navigate the managerial aspects of their roles and contribute to overall effectiveness of health care services.

CHAPTER ONE

MANAGERIAL SKILLS

INTRODUCTION

A manager is an individual who is responsible for staff/employees. A manager directs, supervises, a business or organization, plans, directs, monitors and takes corrective action of individuals or a group of people.

A manager supervises employees and ensures that proper procedures are in place and implemented in order for a smooth practice of Occupational Therapist in the organization ensuring ethical and legal practice.

The manager is responsible for staff recruitment, maintaining active caseload, Departmental representative to a larger organization and the manager must also look into proper staff ratios, educational background, clinical skill of the personnel and the scope of services provided by the organization.

TYPES OF MANAGERIAL SKILLS

PLANNER

PROBLEM SOLVERMANAGERIAL SKILLS ORGANIZER

DIRECTOR

I. PLANNER

Planning is the fundamental step required to achieve a goal of the organization. Planning demands how and when the goal set can be achieved.

Planning gives a brief idea about the objectives of the organization and the actions required to achieve these objectives. Planning is a process of establishing short term and long-term goals that are in relation to the vision and mission of the organization. Here short-term goal can be procuring all the required equipment and employees to run the organization and long term can be taking the organization to reach greater heights like being recognized at the international level. A good planning involves identifying and prioritising the goals of the organization/department.

i.

CHARACTERISTICS OF PLANNING

- Managerial Function
- Goal Oriented
- Continuous Process
- Futuristic
- Decision Making
- Pervasive
- Intellectual Process

- **Managerial Function**

Planning is considered the basic fundamental function, where it includes and provides a base for other functions of the management, i.e. organizing, staffing, directing etc.

- **Goal Directed**

Focusses on defining the goals of the organization and deciding appropriate action and plan that is necessary for reaching the goals.

- **Continuous Process**

Planning is a continuous process and once the set goals are achieved, new goals are set considering the organization's present and future conditions and requirements. The Occupational Therapist manager now focusses on the next goal and how to achieve it.

- **Futuristic**

In the process of planning, the Occupational Therapy manager should also look into the future goals of the organization, so that the organization is well planned to face the upcoming/ future challenges.

- **Decision making**

Decisions are made regarding the choice of alternative course of action that can be undertaken to reach the goal.

- **Pervasive**

Planning is called a pervasive function of management because planning occurs at all levels of management in an organisation, directing all managers in different organization units to work towards achieving the organization goals and objectives.

- **Intellectual Process**

Planning is an intellectual process, as plans are always based on sound judgement. It involves top-level management.

EXAMPLE

Sundar, The Head of The Department of Occupational Therapy, St. Martins Hospital Bangalore. He wants to conduct a workshop regarding the topic 'INFLUENCE OF OT IN GERIRATRICS' This workshop is organised for professionals of various department.

Planning

Here the Head of the Department, Sundar serves as the manager of the entire event. He has to plan the event from the beginning to the end. It may include deciding the venue, setting time schedule, assigning speakers, sending out invitations etc.

Goal directed

Now there is a plan already for conducting the event. Here comes the goals of the Sundar is to make sure that all the steps planned to making this event a success is going smooth and also to ensure that the goals are achieved according to the timeline that has set.

Continuous process

The plan of the event could be modified or replanned by Sundar according to the future needs and considering the suggestions of other members of the organisation or workshop conducting committee.

Futuristic

Furthermore, the Sundar has to be able to answer these questions, the questions which are related to future such as what all events has too included in the workshop, how to manage the time for each event, when to conduct the event so that it might be convenient for all, whom to call to speak based on the experience and knowledge on the given topic. Under planning answer to this question are found out. Hence it is futuristic.

Decision making

If the plan to achieve the goal is obstructed such as the assigned speaker might not be able to arrive on time, then the Sundar should have an alternative way to manage the time schedule.

Pervasive process

Sundar can appoint a student representative so as to supervise the arrangements of the auditorium (i.e.) to prepare posters, pamphlets regarding the topic. The institutional staff can welcome the guest and host the entire event and the HOD (Sundar) who serves as the manager can organise the event as whole.

Intellectual process

In a mental activity a manager decides the goals to be achieved and the actions through which those goals to be achieved.

i.

STRATEGIC PLANNING

Strategic planning can be defined as the method that organizations use to achieve all their goals. Every organization should have a strategic plan. Strategic planning involves documenting the strengths and weaknesses of the organization along with the other opportunities that can be used in the later stages in fulfilling the objective/goal of the organization. For a strategic planning to be successful, the Occupational Therapy manager should use the SWOT analysis where in S stands for Strengths, W for Weakness, O for Opportunities and T for Threats. Once the strengths and weaknesses have been analysed the next step can be prioritizing the goals of the organisation. The goals set should be objective and measurable so as to it can help in attaining the goals of the organization. The manager should start developing a plan to achieve the goals successfully. Developing a plan also involves the measures necessary to attain these objectives and a timeline to achieve these goals should be set. Following developing a plan the next step is to execute the plan. To do so the manager has to communicate the plan with the organization and submit all the relevant documentation to the organization. The final step in strategic planning involves reviewing and revising the plan and to re-evaluate the objective and how far the plan was successful in attaining the goals of the organization.

II.

ORGANIZER

Organizing is the next prominent function after planning. The Occupational Therapy manager as an organizer aims at assigning and organizing human as well as other financial resources to carry out the plan of the organization successfully. It also requires an OT manager to develop good professional relationships with the workers and entails the planning of the task to achieve the goal. The OT manager determines the overall goals of the organization and divides the employees into different departments within the organization.

Example: The employees who have specialized in treating neurological conditions like cerebrovascular accident, traumatic brain injury, Gullian barre syndrome etc and the employees who are good at treating paediatric conditions can be clubbed into one group etc. By doing this, it facilitates in better outcome of the goal of the organization. The OT manager is also responsible for recruiting, training and hiring new staffs.

i. **PROCESS OF ORGANIZING**

1. Determining Targets
2. Determining Actions
3. Co-ordination of Actions
4. Distribution of duties and Responsibilities
5. Assignment of Authority
6. Formation of Organization Charts and Manuals

7.

Organizing Actions

I. **Determining Targets**

The first step in organizing is determining the targets/clients who can benefit from Occupational Therapy services. After determining the targets, they should be based on the short-term and long-term goals of the organization that needs to be achieved.

II. **Determining Actions**

Once the targets are determined, the next step is to determine the actions that can fulfil the goals of the target i.e., the patient, the goals formulated for them etc.

III. **Co-ordination of Actions**

Once the targets and actions are determined, it is necessary to co-ordinate the targets and actions and this can be done by the employee of the organization, who is well versed in handling the goals set for the client.

IV. **Distribution of Duties and Responsibilities**

In distribution of duties and responsibilities, the manager divides the duties based on the distinctive ability and responsibility of the employee and each task must be solely delegated to different employees.

V. **Assignment of Authority**

The therapist must be given the required authority while dealing with patient/client. The therapist should be well aware of the instructions and rules that they are expected to follow while handling a client.

VI. **Formation of Organization Charts and Manuals**

Organization charts and manuals are prepared for the purpose of describing the organisation structure. They are considered as tools of management control. Its purpose is to provide an easy-to- understand visualization of an organization's structure and relationships between its various parts.

Employer making manual for rules and regulations that to be followed by the practitioners and other employees of organization.

VII. Organizing Actions

Organizing actions involves the final output that involves- assigning tasks, grouping tasks into departments, delegating authority, and allocating resources across the organization.

EXAMPLE

A client named Parinika, 5 years old female, diagnosed with Cerebral Palsy, came to the occupational therapy department. Her mother complains of the child not able to sit without support, not able to walk, not using both the hands, not allow to touch face, no eye contact, not able to perform the daily chores.

Determining target

The occupational therapist named Priya was assigned to the patient. The therapist gone through the referrals and found out that the client will be benefited by the occupational therapy services. A complete assessment was taken in the allocated time. Then the therapist set the long- term and short-term goals. Thus, the target has been determined.

Determining action

In order to achieve these goals, Priya set a 45 minutes session with a well-planned therapy programme for every Wednesday and Friday (12.00 -1.00). In addition to home therapy program has been explained to the caretaker and the therapist reviewed it on every session.

Coordination of Actions

If the assigned therapist, Priya is on leave then she should assign the client to another therapist who is specialised in the same field.

Distribution of duties and responsibilities

The head of the department distributes or assign duties/patient to the respective therapist. Therapist Priya, she could plan home therapy and other interventions and distribute duties among caregivers and family as well as others in department.

Assignment of Authority

The assigned therapist Priya must have complete authority to take the detailed assessment of the client and to set a treatment plan. Priya is also authorised to change the plan according to the improvement of the client.

Formation of Organization Charts and Manuals

Head of the Department or Organization making charts depicting the employee's roles to illustrate the reporting relationships and chains of command within the organization. It helps to depict what roles the therapist holds and how therapist has charted the treatment and follows manuals of the organisation.

Organizing Actions

The Head of the Department or organization assigning tasks to Priya, Priya making plans and coordinating the processes among patient, family, caregiver, and organization to facilitate the goals identified in the plan.

ii. **PRINCIPLES OF ORGANIZING**

- **Unity of Objective**

This aims at achieving the main goals of the organization. The action taken to achieve each target from employees who are grouped into different groups based on their skill to achieve the goal of the department of the organization.

- **Division of Labour**

Various tasks are distributed amongst the employees based on their abilities and specialization

By doing this/assigning duties based on the employee capability, the productivity of the organization is being enhanced and the employee can focus on the task he is good at.

- **Span of Management**

The Occupational Therapy manager has the authority to supervise limited number of employees and as there are different organizational levels, the work performed will be base on the authority they have.

- **Co-ordination**

For the goals to be achieved all the employees of the organization should work together as it results in the growth of this organization.

- **Unity of Command**

Unity of Command is explained as only one person taking command over the entire department/organization and the sub-ordinates shall receive only from the commandant

EXAMPLE

Sri Rajendra Memorial Hospital, Occupational Therapy Department consists of 10 clinical therapist and it is governed by the Head of the Department named Dr. Shashikala. In order to run the institution Dr. Shashikala follows the following principles,

Unity of objective

As a manager, for Shashikala it is essential to prioritise effective communication and foster patient care. Dr. Shashikala also maintains the client – patient ratio by obtaining appropriate patient target. The manager supervises the entire team and represent the organisation at various levels

As a clinical therapist it is essential to take the complete assessment of the client and document it appropriately and add a note on the improvement achieved by the client

As an accountant- he / she is responsible for the financial management of the organization and tallying all the expenses, funds available etc.

Division of labour

As a manager- Shashikala plays an important role in planning, organising, negotiating, coordinating etc.

As a therapist- therapist who has specialized in neuro rehabilitation can be assigned cases related to neurological conditions and therapist who has specialized in Paediatrics can be provided with cases like Cerebral Palsy, Mental Retardation, Developmental Disabilities, Autism Spectrum Disorder etc.

Span of management

The dean will be supervising the head of the department

The head of the department will be supervising the staff

The staff will be supervising and guiding the students and the hierarchy goes on.

Coordination

The head of the department conduct a group meeting weekly once which includes all the therapist and discuss regarding the patient cases, share the insights, and ensure that everyone is aligned with the organisation's commitment to patient satisfaction.

Unity of command

The head of the department has the entire authority to command the entire department and the therapist are subjected to follow the command. It directs the therapist to be appropriate in relevant treatment protocol and to be updated in the latest condition of the client.

II. DIRECTOR

Following an organizer, is the OT manager as a director. Directing mainly involves guiding the employees of the organization, providing instruction and leadership, so that the objectives of the organization is met. As a director, the manager can distribute the work among the employees. Identifying the important resources to reach the goal, providing constant mentoring post completion of assigned work, so that the individual can improve while performing in the future. The Occupational Therapy manager is also responsible for writing the policies of the organization and the procedures the employee and the clients are expected to follow during their stay at the hospital. The therapist can also discuss the patient's progress post intervention and if there is requirement of any particular standardized assessments.

i.

ELEMENTS OF DIRECTING

1. Supervision
2. Motivation

3. Leadership
4. Communication

1. SUPERVISION

The Occupational Therapy manager mainly performs the guiding, observing and instructing the employees at work. The manager as a supervisor instructs his employee in the use of available resources in an effective manner so that the objective of the organization is achieved.

2. MOTIVATION

The Occupational Therapy manager should motivate the employees towards the accomplishment of the task.

3. LEADERSHIP

Leadership is defined as the process of creating structural changes, wherein the values, vision and ethics of the individual is integrated into culture of a community as a means of achieving sustainable change. The leader should inculcate self-awareness, self-regulation, self-motivation and social skills. The leader is responsible for guiding the employee. The leader should motivate the employee so as to contribute to the department's betterment. The leader is responsible for guiding the employee.

Characteristics to be a good leader include

- Appreciating a job well done
- Part-time options to increase productivity
- Increase in wages on performing consistently in achieving department objectives.
- Providing job security
- Encouraging employees to learn new skills.
- Providing access to community service organizations.
- Flexible fixed hours to the employees
- Providing challenges and various opportunities within the organization
- The leader should keep in mind regarding staff burnout due to over exhaustion.

There are two types of leaderships:

- *Transformational Leaders*

Transformational Leaders are the leaders who are inspirational and energize their employees. Transformational leaders should inspire to focus and look beyond themselves for the greater good of the group. Transformational Leaders helps the employee to recognize that extra effort pays off. Also, a transformational leader helps staff understand that through problem solving rational solutions to problems can be solved.

- *Transactional Leaders*

Transactional Leadership is a leadership meaning that this type of manager establishes standards and intervenes only if those standards are not met. The leader uses contingent rewards and employees are usually aware of the expectations of the organization. This type of leadership involves individual and group work, determining the capabilities of staff and also monitors the work of the employee and make notes of the errors that occurred during the work.

4. COMMUNICATION

Communication mainly involves exchange of ideas, views and information between the manager and employee or between more than two people. Communication is a key to successful completion of the goal of the Organization. Communication between the therapist and the patient and discussing the current status of the patient and can also discuss the measures to improve the functioning of the client.

EXAMPLE

53years old female patient, Anitha who develops Guillain-Barré syndrome. The patient's initial admitted to acute care until discharge after she achieves her short-term goals and regains independence in activities of daily living (ADLs). The patient presents with progressive bilateral upper and lower limb weakness and impaired motor skills. She was then brought to Sri Rajendra memorial hospital for further rehabilitation services including Occupational therapy, Physiotherapy, Psychology etc.

In Occupational Therapy Department,

Supervision –

The manager / Head of the Department supervises development of treatment plan, ongoing therapy, progress notes, Documentation etc...

Motivation –

The Head of department Dr. Mukesh, Motivates the assigned occupational therapist Deepti as well as the caregivers to perform/treat the patient well and as the goals are achieved, the clients will be happy and satisfied.

Leadership –

The Head of Department, Dr. Mukesh guides and encourages Deepti from handling the treatment of the patient to bringing out improvement in patient. He also finds areas in which both therapists as well as patients feel difficult. He appreciates and corrects the therapist whenever necessary.

Communication –

The Head of Department, Dr. Mukesh tends to Actively listen, involves showing interest in what patients and Deepti have to say, acknowledging that you're listening and understanding, and engaging with them throughout the conversation. It helps in development of trust by therapist and patient to organisation and head of the department.

ii. **IMPORTANCE OF DIRECTING**

The director initiates the action in achieving a specific goal, provides guidance and instruction to his employees, looks into the effective utilization of the resources, provides motivation and ensures productivity and proper co-ordination between the therapist and the patient and helps the patient to cope with change.

IV. **PROBLEM-SOLVER**

The manager as a problem solver should focus on moving forward with a positive attitude irrespective of the problem and by doing this the actual mission of the department is realized. As a problem solver the manager should keep a tab on the stress levels of the employees and should teach them the basic relaxation techniques and breathing techniques to relieve stress. Another way of this can be taking breaks in between working hours when the job gets stressful. To solve the problem the manager can use performance review of the employee so that the manager can sit down with the employee and can discuss with him, his best area of performance during a particular period of time and discussing the areas of performance where the employee could have performed better and can sit together and discuss the solutions to overtake the current obstacle in the path of the employee so as to increase the efficiency of the worker. The performance review can focus on team work, communication skills, problem solving skills, patient satisfaction and optimizing the functional abilities of the client.

CHAPTER TWO

DOCUMENTATION

Documentation is the fundamental and most important function performed by Occupational Therapists to support their intervention. Documentation is a key to communicating Intervention plan and approach with the patient as well as other professionals if we are working as a part of Interdisciplinary team.

CASE STUDY

53-year-old female, named Deepti who was a science lecturer by profession at Mahadeva Institute of Science and Technology (MIST). She suffered from Cerebrovascular accident 2years ago. She went through immediate medical treatments and brought to Gopala Swamy Memorial rehabilitation centre, Chennai for further rehabilitation treatment. Patient was brought to occupational therapy for evaluation and following treatment.

ASSESSMENT:

On assessment, patient is evaluated under various domains and each data obtained is documented by the therapist such as

- Demographic data
- Chief complaints
- History (present, past, family, medical)
- General observation
- Examination (motor component, sensory component, cognitive and perceptual component, psychosocial, functional abilities and Performance of ADLs)

PROBLEM IDENTIFICATION:

The data collected on various domains helps therapist to identify the issues that patient is facing in her day-to-day life.

Here, it was identified as the patient currently has difficulty in performing her activities in daily living (as she faces difficulty in using right side of her upper and lower extremity) mainly eating, grooming, dressing and bathing. She also faces difficulty with hand function (Right upper extremity) and issue with gait pattern. The above recorded evaluation helped the therapist in knowing the difficulties and why the problem has occurred.

TREATMENT PLAN:

By documenting the evaluation helps the therapist in framing an Intervention plan and also the Occupational Therapist could always look back and compare the pre therapy and post therapy results.

Here, therapist initiates therapy by making daily plan for individuals by taking reference from the data documented.

PAYMENT METHOD:

By appropriate documentation allow individuals to effectively use their current health insurance policies or try to implement a new one such that all are able to acquire equal services regardless of their limitations.

Here, the patient was suggested by her insurance company to submit documents from the hospital for reimbursement purpose. Thus, she requested the therapist as well as the management to provide her documents regarding the treatment plan, duration and other details.

REFERRALS:

While working in an interdisciplinary team, this documentation of the findings of the patient will be very useful, while discussing the case with other team members.

Here, seeing the patient file documented by other departments, therapist could easily recognize that what all therapy or treatment are ongoing for the individual. Therapist could also take referral from other departments.

LATER ON, PURPOSES:

- These documents help therapists to compare the pretherapy as well as post therapy status
- To further study on cases
- Research purpose

The documents are reflected at various levels of the organization/ department in the hospital and evaluates the quality of services provided by the organization. The AOTA's Standards of Practice for Occupational

Therapy (2010) states that an Occupational Therapy practitioner documents Occupational Therapy services and abides by the time frames, formats and standards established by the practice settings, Government agencies, external accreditation programs, payers and AOTA documents. The documentation requirements apply to both written and electric form of documentation. Documentation should reflect on the services provided and enough information to ensure that services are delivered in a safe and effective manner.

I. PURPOSE OF DOCUMENTATION

The Documentation of the client's condition is the only evidence of professional decision making. Documentation is the only availability of facts that proves that treatment has taken place, else the patient themselves can say that it is not documented, so it did not happen. Some of the major purpose of documentation is;

1. *It is effective in planning appropriate treatment*

Example: By documenting the complains, concerns, observation and evaluation while planning an intervention for the patient, the therapist can refer at the document, so that therapist can refer the document, so that the therapist does not leave out any concerns of the client.

1. *It stands as a legal document*

The therapist can always use the document containing the client evaluation, intervention, duration of therapy, types of services provided as a legal document, when there is necessity so that the evaluating authorities can rule out if anything went wrong while providing intervention

3. *It is effective during reimbursement*

Patient claiming insurance for reimbursement of the payment paid by client during the services. By having documented details about the patient, the total amount to be reimbursed can be rechecked and provided for the services the patient has paid during the services

4. *Provides communication among the patient, treatment team and family.*

The document comes in handy while discussing therapy plan with the team members responsible for the patient and the patient relatives. By documenting one might be able to know the client's work, interest, values and needs.

5. *For research purpose*

Patient records in occupational therapy serve as a valuable resource for further research in the field. Researchers can use patient record to analyse historical data, evaluate the effectiveness of interventions, track longitudinal outcomes and explore various aspects of patient care. Additionally, patient record support population study, cost benefit analyses and the development of standardised treatment protocols. Leveraging this documentation enhances the understanding of occupational therapy's impact on individuals and contributes to the continual improvement of health care practices. In short, this documentation can be used in both prospective and retrospective ways.

PROSPECTIVE: *Prospective research looks forward, planning and collecting data over time to observe future outcomes. Prospective studies are often used to assess cause-and-effect relationships.*

RETROSPECTIVE:*Retrospective research looks back, analysing existing data to identify relationships or patterns after events have occurred. Retrospective studies are useful for exploring associations and generating hypotheses.*

II.

PROCESS OF DOCUMENTATION

1. **Screening**
2. **Evaluation**
3. **Intervention**
4. **Outcomes**

SCREENING

Screening usually consists of brief initial assessments to determine client's needs for Occupational Therapy evaluation. Through this the therapist can identify the problems and can plan treatment according to the findings and if necessary for other services, the therapist can refer the client to other services.

Screening usually consists of the demographic data, source of referral, precautions and contraindications, the occupational performance of the client in Activities of daily living, work and leisure. Through screening the therapist can also understand the priorities of the client, the targeted goals and reason for seeking Occupational Therapy Services.

EVALUATION

Once the screening is complete, the next step is to focus on the analysis of the screening report so as to identify the factors causing difficulty in performing the activities. Based on the screening report, the therapist can decide on administering the standardized assessments and non-standardized assessments if necessary and also perform an activity analysis to identify the components to work on for the client. Here the therapist can plan for therapeutic intervention, the expected outcomes and also refer for other services if necessary.

A re-evaluation of the patient is necessary to know the if there is any improvement with the intervention that was provided. A re-evaluation can be performed after 2 weeks/1 month of taking therapy. This re-evaluation helps the therapist to compare the pre therapy and post therapy results. Once the goals are achieved the therapist can formulate the next set of goals to be achieved.

INTERVENTION

Intervention plan documents the goals and approaches used during the therapy sessions, the goals achieved and yet to be achieved. The intervention goals should be meaningful to the client and should be measurable. The intervention approaches used should include creating, promoting, maintaining, modifying and restoring the client's occupational performance. Following the intervention, the patient can be planned for discharge, home exercise program and follow-up services. Outcome measures can be used to demonstrate the measurable functional goals of the client.

The progress report then summarizes the intervention and the client's progress towards fulfilment of the goals. In the report, the therapist should document the intervention plan, task/environmental modifications used, assistive/adaptive devices used, client's response towards occupational therapy services and the progress towards achieving the goals.

OUTCOMES

Outcomes is the summary of the treatment; clients have undergone during their stay at hospital/ during the whole duration of therapy. It summarizes the ability of the client to exchange in occupational performance between the initial evaluation and the discontinuation of services. The discharge report includes the demographic data, summary of the intervention, initial date and services, number of sessions, intervention and approaches used, scoring based on standardized and non-standardized assessments, goals achieved etc.

EXAMPLE

A 50 years old male, named Ramaswamy diagnosed with Stroke, (left hemisphere) came to the occupation therapy department. He came with the complaints such as unable to lift objects, unable to eat food with hands, unable to comb, unable to wear shirt, unable to write etc... He was assigned to a therapist named Ali. The further assessment and treatment plan was conducted by the therapist.

Screening

The therapist went through the referrals and had a overview of all such investigations that has been performed regarding the condition of the client. In addition, the therapist also reviewed the treatment protocols that had been performed till date. The therapist had a note on demographic data of the client and relevant history related to the condition. The therapist observed the general appearance and attitude of limb of the client. Furthermore, the therapist had observed the hand function and his ability to perform daily activities. Thus, the therapist can understand in what all domains the client could be benefited by occupational therapy services. And also, client will have an idea regarding referral to other departments, if required.

Evaluation

Therapist, Ali took complete assessment on various domain such as motor, sensory, cognition, perception, balance etc ..The therapist used standardised and non-standardised tool to asses these areas such as FIM scale to asses ADL of the client , Perdue Peg Board to assess the gross motor and fine motor dexterity examination , non-standardised test such as equilibrium and non-equilibrium test to assess balance etc .

Intervention

Therapist Ali framed short term and long-term goal to the client.

Short term goals include reduce spasticity, improve strength, improve hand function

Long term goals include independence in ADL, Improved writing, return to work.

Therapist also included the complete therapy protocol and duration, home exercise program and the date of reassessment.

Outcomes

Includes the summary of treatment:

Demographic data

Initial date and services

No of session

Intervention and approaches used

Scoring of final assessment

Goals achieved

Adaptive equipment given

Environment modification suggestions

Summary of intervention

III. FORMATS FOR DOCUMENTATION

i. POMR

The Problem Oriented Medical Record (POMR) is a structured approach to acquiring a patient's history. Unlike traditional health records, it centres on the patient's problems, their progression and the interconnections between clinical events. POMR aims for an organised, comprehensive, and updated medical record. It offers physician a systematic view of patient's history, aiding in explicit hypothesis formulation and clinical decision making. While there is a focus on implementing information systems for POMR, some challenges exist, such as limitations in handling administrative reports.

PHASES OF POMR:

Phase 1- DATABASE

Gather comprehensive information about the client which includes demographic data, chief complaints, present history, past history, family history, medical history, vocational history, evaluation data etc...

Phase 2- PROBLEM LIST

Identification of a specific problem list from the interpretation of the database, including specific impairment of function (Physical, psychological, social and vocational) resulting from the disease process or from secondary impairments.

Phase 3- PLAN OF ACTION

Identification of a specific plan of care that includes interventions for each of the problems described; evaluative and progress notes are included for each problem.

Phase 4 – NOTES ON PROGRESS

Determination of the effectiveness of the plan of care and subsequent changes as a result of patient progress.

ii. **SOAP NOTES**

The SOAP notes format was first used by Dr. Lawrence Weed in 1970. Each letter in the acronym stands for S- Subjective, O- Objective, A-

Assessment, P- Plan

SUBJECTIVE SECTION

This part includes the information reported by the client, family or caregivers. The information that the client gives about the current state like emotional state, physical state, complaints etc. Client's subjective response to treatment is recorded in this section. Direct quotes can be used when necessary. This section should include relevant information, avoid statements that can be misinterpreted. Behavioural responses can be included if the patient is non-verbal/ poor communication skills.

Example; the patient is a case of cerebrovascular accident and complains that he has difficulty in getting up from bed and feels depressed for being dependent on the family members.

OBJECTIVE SECTION

The therapist documents the results of assessments, tests and measurements performed as well as objective observation. Data that are recorded in the objective section are measurable, quantifiable and observable. Only factual information must be included. Results of standardized and non- standardized tests that are documented in this part of the note. Objective section can be organized categorically. Information that is organized and should follow the categories outlines in Occupational Therapy Practice Framework (OTPF). Number of visits, intervention, Result of Standardized assessments, Caregiver- education, barriers to intervention, Previous intervention/current intervention, short term goals etc. Positive prognostic indicators include ability to follow direction, document in evaluation and re- evaluation notes. Positive prognostic indicators indicate the patient has potential to be independent/ return to work and the prognosis is good. This also includes motivation, following commands and initiating action. Negative prognostic indicators include unresponsive to stimuli, but requires splinting for maintaining joint integrity. Examples of negative prognostic indicators include poor orientation, inability to follow directions, absent or inadequate arousal etc.

ASSESSMENT

Therapist summarizes the subjective and objective findings and interprets the data to establish the most appropriate therapy program. The impairments and functional deficits are analysed and prioritized to determine what impact they have on clients Occupational Performance. Only the information included in subjective and objective section is discussed in the assessment section. The therapist should also document any modification that need to be made for the existing goals. The assessment section should end with a statement justifying the need for continued Occupational Therapy Services.

PLAN

As the client achieves the targeted goals the plan is revised and new goals are established. Documentation reflects the client updated goals as well as any modifications to frequency of therapy. Planning should also involve care giver education, patient education and family interaction.

CASE STUDY

Rahul was a 68-year-old man who underwent a right total hip replacement. After discharge, he has been referred to and was evaluated by occupational therapist. The occupational therapy intervention plan indicated that Rahul would receive occupational therapy 3 days a week until his expected discharge date in 3 weeks. The plan was for Rahul to attain independence in all activities of daily living (ADL) so that he could return to his apartment, where he lived alone.

The second occupational therapy session consisted of reviewing total hip precautions, providing Rahul with assistive devices for dressing, and instructing him in the use of equipment and adapted dressing techniques. The occupational therapist recorded the following occupational therapy treatment note using a SOAP note format:

Nirmala medical college

Occupational Therapy Department

Name: Rahul

IP No: xxxxx90

Date: January 20, 2010

Time: 8:45 a.m.

Subjective:

Client stated, "I need to be able to take care of myself so I can go back home."

Objective:

A 45-minute OT session was administered in Occupational Therapy Department. Client accurately recalled 3/3 fatal hip precautions and was issued a Reacher, long-handle shoehorn, and sock assist. Client was then instructed in use of devices and compensatory methods for lower limb dressing. While sitting on edge of bed, client donned pants over affected lower extremity with moderate assistance and over unaffected leg with minimum assistance using Reacher and dressing stick. Client also required minimum assistance to don socks using sock aid and to don loafers using long-handle shoehorn. Contact guard and use of walker were required for client to stand and pull up clothing.

Client demonstrated good endurance and ability to safely adhere to total hip precautions throughout session.

Assessment:

Excellent potential for ADL independence is evident in client's good endurance and ability to understand and follow instructions. Continuation of Occupational Therapy is recommended to maximize client's self-care abilities and safety for return home.

Plan:

Continue OT 3 times weekly for skilled instruction in lower-body dressing, bathing, and transfers. Next session instruct client in use of transfer tub bench and assistive devices for bathing.

iii. RUMBA

According to Perinchief, this is beneficial in organizing the therapist's thought process for effective documentation.

RUMBAstands for

R- Is the information **Relevant**

U- Is the information **Understandable**

M- Is the information **Measurable**, A way to know how and when the goal was met.

B- Is the information **Behavioural**, the goal/outcome must be seen and heard.

A-Is the outcome **Achievable**, the goal/outcome must be do-able and realistic

iv. SMART

Points to consider:

- Specific: Ask yourself the questions: who, what, when, where and why? What will the patient or caregiver do? Customize the goal for the patient's issue(s). Avoid vague descriptions.
- Measurable: How will I measure progress? How will I know it is achieved? Use validated and objective measures.
- Actionable/Attainable: Is the goal reasonable and achievable? Can this really happen? Set realistic goals for your patient's physical, cognitive, social and environmental barriers.
- Relevant: Why is achieving this goal important? Is the goal meaningful? Avoid goals that are specific to standardized test items. Establish goals in partnership with your patient/caregiver. Focus on function

- Time Bound: When will the goal be achieved? What is the timeframe for achieving the goal? Set a deadline and avoid "by discharge".

ITEM

EXAMPLES

SMART component

Person or Area of Body

Patient, Caregiver or Parent. Head, neck, shoulder, trunk, low back, hip, knee, ankle, hands, finger, etc.

Specific

Impairment

Strength, ROM, balance, coordination, gait, swelling, pain, behaviour, nutrition intake, etc.

Specific

Impairment Goal

ROM degrees, MMT grade, pain VAS level, developmental milestone, etc.

Measurable

Functional Activity

Rolling, sitting, crawling, standing, cruising, walking, transfers, dressing, eating, bathing, etc.

Actionable

Target Performance

Assistance level, cues, trials/opportunities, seconds, minutes, hours, day(s), distance, etc.

Measurable

Rationale

Mobility, play, dressing, ADLs, ensure safety in home, etc.

Relevant

Target Timeframe/Date

Deadline: 2 weeks, 4 weeks, 3 months, 2 visits, et

Time bound

v. COMPUTERISED HEALTH RECORDS

The adoption of the electronic health records (EHRs) in recent years aims to enhance client care, reduce costs and improve efficiency in the health care system. EHRs offer benefit such as space efficiency, legible documentation, streamlined procedures, faster communication, and reduced errors. The are particularly advantages for remote health care settings, allowing immediate data submission and easy access to client information. Specialised software tailored to occupational therapy practices further contributes to organizational efficiency. Computerised health records take up much less storage than traditional paper records. They are type written so errors due to mistakes in penmanship or poor handwriting are minimised.

The requirement for occupational therapy practitioners (and other healthcare providers) to log in and log out of the system, even for short absences, is rooted in principles of patient confidentiality, data security, and accountability.

1.Patient Confidentiality: Logging in and out of the system ensures that patient health records are secure and only accessible by authorized personnel. This is crucial for maintaining patient confidentiality and complying with privacy regulations.

2.Accountability and Auditing: Each time a practitioner accesses a client's health record, writes a note, or makes corrections, these actions are logged under their unique identifier or "signature." This accountability helps in tracking who has accessed the information and when, which is essential for auditing purposes.

3.Preventing Unauthorized Access: Requiring login/logout for short absences helps prevent unauthorized access to patient records. It ensures that no one can access sensitive health information in the practioner's absence, even for a brief period.

4.Data Integrity: The practice of logging in and out contributes to the integrity of the health record system. It ensures that actions taken within the system are attributed to the responsible individual, promoting transparency and accuracy in the documentation process.

CHAPTER THREE

MARKETING

INTRODUCTION

Marketing is the ability to understand and appropriately apply the business skills and is a key component in development of successful private practice. Marketing is one of the business skills Occupational Therapists need to have in order to take full advantage of the opportunities available to entrepreneurs in health care. In the present scenario, it is the basic necessity that an Occupational Therapist must have to reach people through the services using marketing. For marketing, the individual must first identify the target group/clients who can benefit from the services and analyse the needs, evaluating if their needs are appropriate and implementing them using various marketing strategies. This can be depicted using a flow chart.

Occupational Therapist

Identifying the target population

Goals of the Client

Analysing their needs

Evaluating to know if the Occupational Therapist can provide those services

Choosing the appropriate marketing strategy

Finalising the budget for marketing

Implementation of the strategy

Conducting a survey to know the reach

Changing the marketing strategy if it did not fulfil the estimated reach

There are various marketing strategies that an Occupational Therapist can use to market their services. Marketing used to be centered around traditional marketing techniques including television, radio, mail, and in-person marketing etc. Currently the world has expanded to advance technology and marketing can be done from the place you are in through social media, content making and e-mails.

Marketing can be divided into two types:

I. *Traditional Marketing Techniques*

i. In-person Marketing
v. Electronic Media Marketing
v. Outdoor Marketing
v. Print Marketing
v. Event Marketing

II. *Digital Marketing Techniques*

v. E-mail Marketing
v. Blogging
v. Video Marketing
v. Content Making
v. Search Engine Optimization
v. Paid Ads

I. TRADITIONAL MARKETING TECHNIQUES

Traditional Marketing Techniques were in most use until the early 2000. Before the internet and technology was available. Traditional marketing was a primary source the organizational companies would use to maximize their reach. These techniques are used at present but is less compared to the marketing using technology.

i. In-Person Marketing

In-person Marketing can be otherwise known as direct marketing. This type of marketing involves delivering specific content to the potential clients. Direct marketing mediums can include

- Vouchers for free
- Catalogue distribution
- Coupon distribution
- Pamphlets

Example: Pamphlets can be provided at places where there is a potential crowd like at market, malls etc. In these pamphlets one can write the services they offer and how it can benefit the potential clients.

ii. **Electronic Media Marketing**

Electronic Media Marketing mainly involves the use of television and radios for advertising. In this, the organization can convey information through visual or auditory media which will grab the attention of the client/ viewers better. By using mode of television an organization can advertise their services provided and the benefit the potential client can get.

Example: Recording the patient talking about Occupational Therapy and how our services have benefitted. The patient can be asked to talk about their journey with Occupational Therapy and talking about their pre therapy and post therapy state.

iii. **Outdoor Marketing**

Outdoor Marketing from the name it suggests marketing is done on the outside. This can be achieved through the public display of advertising outside of the target population houses. The public display can also be done at the places, where the clients are most likely to visit. Outdoor marketing can include printed advertisement on benches, sticker wraps on vehicles, advertisements on public transit etc.

Example: Occupational Therapist should advertise regarding their services and what an Occupational Therapist can do. Gathering in market and performing street play to convey to people the significance of our services.

iv. **Print Marketing**

Print Marketing usually replicate small, easily printed content, that does not consume much time. Traditionally the Occupational Therapists can mass produce the printed materials and the printed content will be completely similar to all the clients.

Examples include:

- Brochure
- Business Cards
- Billboards
- Newspaper Ads
- Posters
- Printed Banners

Example: Occupational Therapy Practitioner can provide their visiting cards to different doctors at various hospitals. Another example can be Occupational Therapist going to the potential doctors like Orthopedist, Geriatrician, Neurologist, Pediatrician etc and providing them with brochures and educating them about Occupational Therapy services so that they can refer potential cases.

v. **Event Marketing**

Event Marketing entails gathering a group of people, i.e. the potential clients at a specific location and how Occupational Therapists provides services and the services that are available in that particular organization and they can approach an Occupational Therapist when there is a necessity. Some examples include trade shows, conferences, seminars, private event etc.

Example: Occupational Therapist attending conferences conducted by Department of Psychiatry and talking about Occupational Therapy Role in mental health. Attending conference conducted by Department of Pediatrics and educating them about Occupational Therapy Role in pediatric condition like cerebral palsy, down syndromes, developmental delay, sensory processing disorder etc.

II. **DIGITAL MARKETTING STRATEGIES**

Digital Marketing techniques are in the current trends and the term digital marketing refers to the use of digital channels to market the services. Digital marketing is a component of marketing that uses the internet and online based technologies and uses digital media platforms to promote their services.

Some of the Digital Marketing techniques include-

i. **E-mail Marketing**

E-mail marketing allows an individual to directly send information to client who can benefit from Occupational Therapy services. Some tips to improve E-mail marketing include

- Use striking subject lines to encourage people to open your e-mail.
- Personalize E-mail by using their names in the E-mail.
- Mentioning the organizations brand style throughout the e-mail.
- Targeting subscribers to send most relevant contents.

ii. **Blogging**

Blogging enables an individual to share helpful information with clients who actively seek it.

Some ways to improve blogging include

- Posting content often
- Writing for the clients
- Using relevant key words
- Using content calendar to stay organized with posting content.

iii. **Video Marketing**

Videos help a therapist to deliver abundance of information in less time. Videos have highest percentage of reaching individuals in less time. The following ways can be followed to launch successful strategy.

- Posting different videos like tutorial short clips.
- Posting videos often on social media to maximize reach.
- Scheduling the content to post on social media.
- Replying in the comments section to the people who have commented on the post or video.

iv. **Content Making**

Sharing valuable contents on social media can boost the engagement. Social media marketing enables an Occupational Therapist to have direct connection with the potential clients and deliver relevant information straight to them. An Occupational Therapist can connect with clients on various social platforms including Twitter, Facebook, LinkedIn, Instagram, Pinterest.

Following ways can be used to launch a successful social media strategy.

- Posting contents often to ensure followers see your content.
- Engaging with clients to build relationship.
- Posting variety and diverse content that can be accessible and appealing to maximum member of the audience.

v. **Search Engine Optimization**

When people want to find Occupational Therapy services the turn search engine to help them find the right one. To optimize the search engine, search engine optimization can help. Tips to rank higher in relevant search results include-

- Optimizing title tags to ensure they are informative when people click.
- Identify relevant key words and integrate them to the site.
- Integrate design to deliver mobile friendly experience.
- Improving sites load time to help deliver information to your audience fast.

vi.

Paid Ads

Pay per click advertising is an excellent way to reach people choosing an Occupational Therapist. Few ways to launch a successful PPC strategy include: -

- Using negative key words to prevent Ads from appearing in relevant search results.
- Using Ad extension

MARKETING IMPLICATIONS IN OCCUPATIONAL THERAPY

Marketing entails steps similar to planning the managers, first evaluates and analyzes the needs of the patient and then develop the marketing strategy and implements it. Occupational Therapist can first collect information by reviewing the medical records, examining the age, income, location and then reviewing the marketing strategy and gathering data if the used marketing strategy is maximizing reach. Promotion of Occupational Therapy services can be done through marketing techniques discussed earlier. Occupational Therapy managers can incorporate marketing into achieving the goals by using proved marketing strategies. The Occupational Therapy managers must educate the staff regarding advantage of marketing. The employees can be reminded of the impression they can create while providing their services.

CHAPTER-3

MARKETING

INTRODUCTION

Marketing is the ability to understand and appropriately apply the business skills and is a key component in development of successful private practice. Marketing is one of the business skills Occupational Therapists need to have in order to take full advantage of the opportunities available to entrepreneurs in health care. In the present scenario, it is the basic necessity that an Occupational Therapist must have to reach people through the services using marketing. For marketing, the individual must first identify the target group/clients who can benefit from the services and analyse the needs, evaluating if their needs are appropriate and implementing them using various marketing strategies. This can be depicted using a flow chart.

Occupational Therapist

Identifying the target population

Goals of the Client

Analysing their needs

Evaluating to know if the Occupational Therapist can provide those services

Choosing the appropriate marketing strategy

Finalising the budget for marketing

Implementation of the strategy

Conducting a survey to know the reach

Changing the marketing strategy if it did not fulfil the estimated reach

There are various marketing strategies that an Occupational Therapist can use to market their services. Marketing used to be centered around traditional marketing techniques including television, radio, mail, and in-person marketing etc. Currently the world has expanded to advance technology and marketing can be done from the place you are in through social media, content making and e-mails.

Marketing can be divided into two types:

I. *Traditional Marketing Techniques*

i. In-person Marketing
v. Electronic Media Marketing
v. Outdoor Marketing
v. Print Marketing
v. Event Marketing

II. *Digital Marketing Techniques*

v. E-mail Marketing
v. Blogging

v. Video Marketing
v. Content Making
v. Search Engine Optimization
v. Paid Ads

I. TRADITIONAL MARKETING TECHNIQUES

Traditional Marketing Techniques were in most use until the early 2000. Before the internet and technology was available. Traditional marketing was a primary source the organizational companies would use to maximize their reach. These techniques are used at present but is less compared to the marketing using technology.

i. In-Person Marketing

In-person Marketing can be otherwise known as direct marketing. This type of marketing involves delivering specific content to the potential clients. Direct marketing mediums can include

- Vouchers for free
- Catalogue distribution
- Coupon distribution
- Pamphlets

Example: Pamphlets can be provided at places where there is a potential crowd like at market, malls etc. In these pamphlets one can write the services they offer and how it can benefit the potential clients.

ii. **Electronic Media Marketing**

Electronic Media Marketing mainly involves the use of television and radios for advertising. In this, the organization can convey information through visual or auditory media which will grab the attention of the client/ viewers better. By using mode of television an organization can advertise their services provided and the benefit the potential client can get.

Example: Recording the patient talking about Occupational Therapy and how our services have benefitted. The patient can be asked to talk about their journey with Occupational Therapy and talking about their pre therapy and post therapy state.

iii. **Outdoor Marketing**

Outdoor Marketing from the name it suggests marketing is done on the outside. This can be achieved through the public display of advertising outside of the target population houses. The public display can also be done at the places, where the clients are most likely to visit. Outdoor marketing can include printed advertisement on benches, sticker wraps on vehicles, advertisements on public transit etc.

Example: Occupational Therapist should advertise regarding their services and what an Occupational Therapist can do. Gathering in market and performing street play to convey to people the significance of our services.

iv. **Print Marketing**

Print Marketing usually replicate small, easily printed content, that does not consume much time. Traditionally the Occupational Therapists can mass produce the printed materials and the printed content will be completely similar to all the clients.

Examples include:

- Brochure
- Business Cards
- Billboards
- Newspaper Ads
- Posters
- Printed Banners

Example: Occupational Therapy Practitioner can provide their visiting cards to different doctors at various hospitals. Another example can be Occupational Therapist going to the potential doctors like Orthopedist, Geriatrician, Neurologist, Pediatrician etc and providing them with brochures and educating them about Occupational Therapy services so that they can refer potential cases.

v. **Event Marketing**

Event Marketing entails gathering a group of people, i.e. the potential clients at a specific location and how Occupational Therapists provides services and the services that are available in that particular organization and they can approach an Occupational Therapist when there is a necessity. Some examples include trade shows, conferences, seminars, private event etc.

Example: Occupational Therapist attending conferences conducted by Department of Psychiatry and talking about Occupational Therapy Role in mental health. Attending conference conducted by Department of Pediatrics and educating them about Occupational Therapy Role in pediatric condition like cerebral palsy, down syndromes, developmental delay, sensory processing disorder etc.

II. **DIGITAL MARKETTING STRATEGIES**

Digital Marketing techniques are in the current trends and the term digital marketing refers to the use of digital channels to market the services. Digital marketing is a component of marketing that uses the internet and online based technologies and uses digital media platforms to promote their services.

Some of the Digital Marketing techniques include-

i. **E-mail Marketing**

E-mail marketing allows an individual to directly send information to client who can benefit from Occupational Therapy services. Some tips to improve E-mail marketing include

- Use striking subject lines to encourage people to open your e-mail.
- Personalize E-mail by using their names in the E-mail.
- Mentioning the organizations brand style throughout the e-mail.

- Targeting subscribers to send most relevant contents.

ii. **Blogging**

Blogging enables an individual to share helpful information with clients who actively seek it.

Some ways to improve blogging include

- Posting content often
- Writing for the clients
- Using relevant key words
- Using content calendar to stay organized with posting content.

iii. **Video Marketing**

Videos help a therapist to deliver abundance of information in less time. Videos have highest percentage of reaching individuals in less time. The following ways can be followed to launch successful strategy.

- Posting different videos like tutorial short clips.
- Posting videos often on social media to maximize reach.
- Scheduling the content to post on social media.

- Replying in the comments section to the people who have commented on the post or video.

iv. **Content Making**

Sharing valuable contents on social media can boost the engagement. Social media marketing enables an Occupational Therapist to have direct connection with the potential clients and deliver relevant information straight to them. An Occupational Therapist can connect with clients on various social platforms including Twitter, Facebook, LinkedIn, Instagram, Pinterest.

Following ways can be used to launch a successful social media strategy.

- Posting contents often to ensure followers see your content.
- Engaging with clients to build relationship.
- Posting variety and diverse content that can be accessible and appealing to maximum member of the audience.

v. Search Engine Optimization

When people want to find Occupational Therapy services the turn search engine to help them find the right one. To optimize the search engine, search engine optimization can help. Tips to rank higher in relevant search results include-

- Optimizing title tags to ensure they are informative when people click.
- Identify relevant key words and integrate them to the site.
- Integrate design to deliver mobile friendly experience.
- Improving sites load time to help deliver information to your audience fast.

vi.

Paid Ads

Pay per click advertising is an excellent way to reach people choosing an Occupational Therapist. Few ways to launch a successful PPC strategy include: -

- Using negative key words to prevent Ads from appearing in relevant search results.
- Using Ad extension

MARKETING IMPLICATIONS IN OCCUPATIONAL THERAPY

Marketing entails steps similar to planning the managers, first evaluates and analyzes the needs of the patient and then develop the marketing strategy and implements it. Occupational Therapist can first collect information by reviewing the medical records, examining the age, income, location and then reviewing the marketing strategy and gathering data if the used marketing strategy is maximizing reach. Promotion of Occupational Therapy services can be done through marketing techniques discussed earlier. Occupational Therapy managers can incorporate marketing into achieving the goals by using proved marketing strategies. The Occupational Therapy managers must educate the staff regarding advantage of marketing. The employees can be reminded of the impression they can create while providing their services.

CHAPTER FOUR

FINANCIAL MANAGEMENT

INTRODUCTION

Financial Management can be defined as planning, organizing, directing and controlling the financial activities such as procurement and utilization of the funds of the organization. The finances are dependent on the combined efforts of the staff at all levels. The managers should be able to develop, define and evaluate the financial goals of the organization. Financial management can improve the quality of health care by providing a system that makes service reasonable at all costs.

OBJECTIVES OF FINANCIAL MANAGEMENT

- The Occupational Therapy manager should ensure the availability of the funds in the organizations and ensure adequate supply of funds.
- The Occupational Therapy manager should use the funds in an effective manner to benefit the organization and to achieve the goals of the organization.
- The Occupational Therapy manager should be able to decide how much fund is required for a particular work and how to distribute/divide the funds within the organization based on the level of importance in fulfilling the goals of the organization.

I. REIMBURSEMENT

Reimbursement refers to the repayment or compensation for expenses incurred. Health insurance is a financial management that provides coverage for medical expense and way of reimbursement in health care.

The Occupational Therapy manager should be knowledgeable about the reimbursement issues and should know the rules and have awareness about the services which are eligible for reimbursement. The eligible services should be stated in the reimbursement document of the organization. The reimbursement loss should be clear and stated utmost clarity. While providing reimbursement the inclusion and exclusion criteria for the given population should be mentioned. The laws should clearly state the reimbursement policy and justification about the denial of reimbursement for particular Occupational Therapy services. The reimbursement policy should also include the appeal mechanism that the client can use for reimbursement.

i. IMPORTANCE OF REIMBURSEMENT

Choosing an insurance plan is crucial for patients as it directly impacts health care reimbursement. A well-selected plan can significantly reduce out-of-pocket cost, ensuring that patients bear a fair share of health care expenses. By understanding the coverage details, including deductibles, copayments and coinsurance, individuals can make informed decisions to minimize their financial responsibility for medical services.

i. INSURANCE POLICIES AROUND THE GLOBE

In US access to payment for health care are controlled by varies policies such as federal and state regulations, private insurance company, employer choice, provider rules and consumer choice. According to US Census Bureau, 27.6 million American Adults are uninsured (2022). Therefore, OT services are limited to those who are uninsured as well as to those who are not aware of OT intervention.

US GOVERNMENT PAYERS

Some of the US Key government payers include:

- **MEDICARE**

Medicare is a federal health insurance program for "people who are 65 or older, people under 65 with certain disabilities and people of any age with end stage renal disease (ESR) ". Medicare consist of four main parts:

- A (inpatient or hospital insurance)
- B (outpatient or medical insurance)
- C (Medicare advantage)
- D (prescription coverage)

MEDICARE IN OT

The role of occupational therapy significantly expanded with the introduction of Medicare in 1965. Initially focused on acute care hospitals, Medicare broadened OT services to non-acute care settings, benefiting individuals over 65 years. In 1970's, services extended to those under 65 with long term disabilities. Advocacy efforts, including state licensure by the American Occupational Therapy Association (AOTA), facilitated OT growth in home health. The 1980's saw OT practitioners utilizing part B outpatient benefits, and despite reimbursement challenges, the Balanced Budget Act secured OT's distinct cap for outpatient services. Today, Medicare remains crucial for OT, influencing private insurance reimbursement and shaping the profession. Continued adaptability is essential as health care dynamics evolve.

- **MEDICAID**

Medicaid, or Title XIX of the Social Security Act, was enacted in 1965, is a federal state program providing health services to individuals with limited incomes. States receive federal matching funds, determined by a formula comparing per capita income levels. Medicaid covers two categories

- Mandatory services
- Optional services

MANDATORY SERVICES

Mandatory services are one that qualify for federal matching funds which must provide by the state or regulatory board. They include inpatient and outpatient, physician early and periodic screening diagnosis, treatment for people younger than 21 years, laboratory work and X-RAY, nursing facilities, occupational therapy, pregnancy related, pediatric, early intervention and immunization services.

OPTIONAL SERVICES

Optional services include rehabilitation (including occupational therapy), diagnostic, orthotic and prosthetics, drugs, home and community-based care for chronic condition, transportation, optometric and eye glasses and hospice care services.

MEDICAID IN OT

Occupational Therapy is one of the optional services; therefore, in some states, OT might not be a covered benefit. However, even in states where OT is included as an optional benefit, states have minimized the benefit by limiting the number of therapy visits or by cutting fee schedule rates for services. The services which Medicaid in occupational therapy include

1. Early and Periodic Screening, Diagnostic and Treatment (EPSDT): Medicaid provides comprehensive services for children under EPSDT. Focusses on preventive and therapeutic care for individuals under the age of 21.
2. Adult Medicaid Services: occupational therapy services for adults are typically covers under Medicaid.
3. Home and Community Based Services (HCBS): some states offer HCBS waivers, allowing Medicaid to cove occupational therapy services provided in a home or community setting rather than in a health care facility.

4.

Coverage For Specific Condition: Medicaid may cover occupational therapy for disabilities, medical condition or injuries as long as the services are deemed medically necessary.

UAE HEALTH INSURANCE SERVICES

Health insurance policy is mandatory in UAE which provide health care services to both residents and non-residents in UAE. The DHA made it mandatory for all the UAE residents to be insured by June 13 2016. This includes not just individuals but also their dependents. No visa is issued if the individual is not insured. In 2018 UAE was ranked one of the top 10 most efficient health care systems in the world. The UAE has a comprehensive, government funded health care system and a rapidly developing private sector that delivers a high standard of care. Health care is regulated at both the federal and emirate level.

Public healthcare services are administered by different regulatory authorities throughout the UAE: the Ministry of Health and Prevention,

Health Authority-Abu Dhabi (HAAD), the Dubai Health Authority (DHA), and the Emirates Health Authority (EHA).

In general, public healthcare covers the following basic health needs:

- Emergencies
- maternity services
- basic health care services (general examinations, diagnostic and treatment services by general practitioners, specialists, and consultants; laboratory services; radiology diagnostic services; physiotherapy services; prescribed drugs and other medicines)
- preventive services (essential vaccinations and immunizations for children and newborns)

Things that are excluded:

- dental and gum exams
- hearing and vision aids
- vision correction by surgery or laser

In the UAE, healthcare coverage is mandatory, and if the employer doesn't offer private health insurance, the employee can obtain it independently. While private health insurance in the UAE tends to be costly, it provides high-quality care. These insurance policies usually encompass a variety of services and treatments, ensuring comprehensive coverage for medical needs. The costs of health insurance vary depending on factors such as coverage extent, provider, and individual factors, so it's advisable to explore different plans to find one that suits your needs and budget.

COVERAGE OF OCCUPATIONAL THERAPY SERVICES

Private health insurance in UAE is offered by various health insurance companies and each company has a variety of plans which differ in offering health care facilities. Occupational therapy services may or may not include in these various insurance plans as plans are opted by the employers or individuals depending on their needs. However, if one requires occupational therapy services, they can opt insurance policies which include this service.

INDIAN HEALTH INSURANCE SERVICES

Health is a human right. It's accessibility and affordability has to be ensured. The escalating cost of medical treatment in India is beyond the reach of common man. While well to do segment of the population both in Rural and Urban areas have accessibility and affordability towards medical care, the same cannot be said about the people who belong to the poor segment of the society.

Health care has always been a problem area for India, a nation with a large population and larger percentage of this population living in urban slums and in rural area, below the poverty line. The government and people have started exploring various health financing options to manage problem arising out of increasing cost of care and changing epidemiological pattern of diseases.

Health insurance is very well established in many countries, but in India it still remains an untapped market. Less than 15% of India's 1.1 billion people are covered through health insurance. And most of it covers only government employees. At any given point of time, 40 to 50 million people are on medication for major sickness and share of public financing in total health care is just about 1% of GDP. Over 80% of health financing is private financing, much of which is out of pocket payments and not by any pre-payment schemes. Given the health financing and demand scenario, health insurance has a wider scope in present day situation in India. However, it requires careful and significant efforts to tap Indian health insurance market with proper understanding and training.

Approximately 514 million people across India were covered under health insurance schemes in 2021, which merely covers 37% of the people in the country. Nearly 400 million individuals in India have zero access to health insurance.

IMPACT OF HEALTH INSURANCE IN OCCUPATIONAL THERAPY

As mentioned above health insurance is not much prevalent in India, the client as well as therapist may face major issues to avail reimbursement for occupational therapy services.

1. Without adequate insurance coverage, clients may bear the full cost of occupational therapy services. This financial burden can be particularly challenging for those with chronic conditions or requiring ongoing therapy.

2. Limited insurance coverage may discourage individuals from seeking occupational therapy due to financial concerns. This reduced accessibility could hinder timely intervention and impact treatment outcomes.

3. Therapists may face challenges in sustaining their practice if clients are unable to afford services without insurance support. This can affect the availability and quality of occupational therapy services.

4. There's a need for increased advocacy and awareness campaigns to highlight the importance of occupational therapy and to push for its inclusion in health insurance coverage. This involves collaboration between healthcare professionals, associations, and policymakers.

5. Encouraging discussions with insurance regulators and providers to revise policies and recognize the value of occupational therapy can contribute to improving reimbursement options.
6. Occupational therapy associations can play a crucial role in advocating for policy changes, promoting awareness, and supporting therapists and clients in navigating the challenges associated with insurance coverage.

INDIAN SCHEMES AND POLICIES

i.

Rashtriya Vayoshri Yojana (RVY)

Rashtriya Vayoshri Yojana (RVY) is a scheme for providing Physical Aids and Assisted-living Devices for Senior citizens belonging to BPL category. This is a Central Sector Scheme, fully funded by the Central Government. The expenditure for implementation of the scheme will be met from the "Senior Citizens' Welfare Fund". The Scheme will be implemented through the sole implementing agency - Artificial Limbs Manufacturing Corporation (ALIMCO), a PSU under the Ministry of Social Justice and Empowerment.

Senior Citizens over age of 60, belonging to BPL category and suffering from any of the age-related disability/infirmity viz. Low vision, Hearing impairment, Loss of teeth and Locomotor disability will be provided with such assisted-living devices which can restore near normalcy in their bodily functions, overcoming the disability/infirmity manifested. The Scheme is expected to benefit all Senior Citizens across the country.

Free of cost distribution of the devices, commensurate with the extent of disability/infirmity that is manifested among the eligible senior citizens.

In case of multiple disabilities/infirmities manifested in the same person, the assistive devices will be given in respect of each disability/ impairment.

Artificial Limbs Manufacturing Corporation (ALIMCO) will undertake one-year free maintenance of the aids & assisted living devices.

Beneficiaries in each district will be identified by the State Governments/UT Administrations through a Committee chaired by the Deputy Commissioner/District Collector.

As far as possible, 30% of the beneficiaries in each district shall be women.

The State Government/UT Administration/District Level Committee can also utilize the data of BPL beneficiaries receiving Old Age Pension under the NSAP or any other Scheme of the State/UT for identification of senior citizens belonging to BPL category.

The devices will be distributed in Camp mode.

Documents required

- Aadhaar /Proof of identity - Passport, Voter ID, Driving license
- Proof of BPL status - certificate from the District Authority for eligibility / BPL ration card / proof of receiving Old Age Pension under Indira Gandhi National Old Age Pension Scheme (IGNOAPS) under the National Social Assistance Programme (NSAP) / Any other Pension Scheme of the State/UT Government for Senior citizens belonging to BPL category
- Certificate from the Medical Officer required for loss of vision, hearing impairment, loss of teeth and locomotor disability requiring use of wheelchair.

Devices supported

Under the Scheme, the following Aids and Assisted-Living Devices will be provided to eligible elderly beneficiary senior citizens, depending upon their physical impairment.

- Walking sticks

- Elbow crutches
- Walkers / Crutches
- Tripods / Quadpods
- Hearing Aids
- Wheelchair
- Artificial Dentures
- Spectacles

ii.

Artificial Limbs Manufacturing Corporation of India (ALIMCO)

Artificial Limbs Manufacturing Corporation of India (ALIMCO) is a Schedule 'C' Minorant Category II Central Public Sector Enterprises, registered under Section 8 (Not for Profit motive) of the Companies Act 2013, (corresponding to Section 25 of the Companies Act, 1956) is functioning under the Administrative Control of Ministry of Social Justice & Empowerment, Department of Empowerment of Persons with Disabilities. It is 100% owned Govt. of India Central Public Sector Enterprises with an objective of benefiting the persons with disability to the maximum extent possible by manufacturing Rehabilitation Aids for persons with disabilities and by promoting, encouraging and developing the availability, use, supply and distribution of Artificial Limbs and other Rehabilitation Aids to the disabled persons of the country. Profitability is not the motive of the operations of the Corporation and its main thrust is in providing better quality of Aids & Appliances to larger number of disabled persons at reasonable price.

The Corporation started manufacturing artificial aids in 1976. It has five Auxiliary Production Centre's (AAPCs) situated at Bhubaneswar (Orissa), Jabalpur (Madhya Pradesh), Bengaluru (Karnataka), Mohali (Punjab), Ujjain (Madhya Pradesh) and Faridabad (Haryana). The Corporation has five Marketing Centre's at New Delhi, Kolkata, Mumbai, Hyderabad & Guwahati.

In endeavor to enhance outreach of benefits of ADIP scheme by providing aids and assistive devices to Persons with Disabilities across the country, ALIMCO has started the opening of RRCs at National Institutes (NIs) and Satellite/ Regional Centers working under Deep'd, Govt. of India on PAN India basis.

The Corporation is the only manufacturing company producing various types of assistive devices under one roof to serve all types of disabilities across the country.

iii.

Assistance To Disabled Person for Purchase / Fitting of Aids/ Appliances (ADIP):

The Assistance to Disabled Persons for Purchase of Fitting Aids and Appliances (ADIP) Scheme is a grant-in-aid initiative in India. It aims to assist individuals with disabilities in acquiring durable, sophisticated, and scientifically manufactured aids and appliances. The scheme is implemented through various agencies, including National Institutes, Composite Regional centers, Artificial Limbs Manufacturing Corporation of India (ALIMCO), District Disability Rehabilitation centers, State Handicapped Development Corporations, local bodies, and non-governmental organizations (NGOs).

The key objectives of the ADIP Scheme are:

1. Aid Provision: Provide financial assistance to eligible agencies for the procurement of modern, standard aids and appliances.
2. Rehabilitation Support: Facilitate physical, social, and psychological rehabilitation of persons with disabilities by mitigating the effects of their disabilities.
3. Economic Empowerment: Enhance the economic potential of individuals with disabilities by ensuring access to appropriate assistive devices.
4. Diversity of Implementing Agencies: Involve a range of entities, including national and regional institutes, manufacturing corporations, district rehabilitation centers, state development corporations, local bodies, and NGOs, to effectively reach and support people with disabilities across different regions.
5. Focus on Scientifically Manufactured Devices: Emphasize the procurement of aids and appliances that are scientifically manufactured, durable, and in adherence to established standards.

Overall, the ADIP Scheme plays a crucial role in promoting inclusivity, independence, and improved quality of life for persons with disabilities by providing them with essential assistive devices. The focus on diverse implementing agencies ensures a widespread and comprehensive reach to address the varied needs of the disabled population.

iv. *NATIONAL HANDICAPPED FINANCE DEVELOPMENT COORPORATION (NHFDC)*

The National Handicapped Finance and Development Corporation (NHFDC) is a government organization in India that aims to promote economic and development activities for the benefit of people with disabilities.The Corporation is registered under section 25 of the Companies Act, 1956 (Corresponding provisions of section 8 of the Companies Act, 2013) on 24.01.1997 as a company not for profit. It provides financial assistance, scholarships, and skill development programs to empower individuals with disabilities and enhance their socio-economic status. The NHFDC plays a crucial role in supporting inclusive initiatives and fostering opportunities for people with disabilities to lead independent and productive lives.

National Divyangjan Finance and Development Corporation (NDFDC) is mandated to work for the Socio-economic empowerment of PW Ds. There are two flagship schemes of NDFDC for channelizing concessional loan through its partner agencies i.e.

- Divyangjan Swavalamban Yojana (DSY)- which is individual centric. The main objective of this scheme is to assist the needly disabled persons by providing concessional loan for economic and overall empowerment.

- Vishesh Microfinance Yojana (VMY)- which is for Self Help Groups / Joint liability groups through various partner agencies for the welfare and rehabilitation of Persons with Disabilities in the country.

v. ***NIRAMAYA (Health Insurance Scheme)***

The objective of Niramaya scheme is to provide affordable Health Insurance to persons with Autism, Cerebral Palsy, Mental Retardation and Multiple Disabilities. All enrolled beneficiaries will get a health insurance cover of up to Rs. 1.0 lakh as defined in the chart OPD treatment including the medicines, pathology, diagnostic tests, etc., Regular Medical checkup for non-ailing disabled, Dental Preventive Dentistry, Surgery to prevent further aggravation of disability, Non- Surgical/ Hospitalization, Corrective Surgeries for existing Disability including congenital disability, Ongoing Therapies to reduce impact of disability and disability related complications, Alternative Medicine and Transportation costs.

i.

Swavlamban Health Insurance

This policy is a group plan, where the family members of the specially-abled individual are also covered. If the individual is suffering from a disability such as blindness or deafness, this policy can be beneficial. This policy also does not require any medical tests. If the annual family income is less than Rs.3 Lakhs, they are eligible for this policy. The premium is Rs.3100, of which only 10% has to be paid by the policyholder; the remainder is paid by the government.

II. BUDGETING

Budgeting is an important factor in the financial management of the organization. The budget should be expressed in numerical and a fixed budget should be decided on a particular service and the budget should be divided equally based on the importance of goals. The budget is an estimate the present and future needs and the previous records of the planned budget, expended budget should be available. Comparison of the previous budget, current budget and future budget should be made so as to determine the increase/decrease in the planned budget. Budgets when planned should be flexible enough so as to allow room for the unexpected demands on the organization by a particular department in the organization. The budget proposed for the month should be discussed with the higher officials of the organization. It is important for Occupational Therapy manager to be knowledgeable about the financial management without which the manager cannot justify fees for service, staffing, department budget etc.

i. TYPES OF BUDGETING

1. Master Budget

- Department Budget
- Capital Budget

2. Revenue, Expense and Operating Budget

1. **MASTER BUDGET**

Master Budget as the name suggests is the budget for the entire organization. This master budget is usually provided to the higher officials of the organization like the Trustees of the organization and the official at top level management. The budget to the department is indicated but only in terms of revenues and expenses.

1. **Departmental Budget**

Departmental Budget is a part of master budget and these indicate the budget required for every individual department within the organization. Based on the level of importance of the budget required for a particular unit within the department the budget can be categorized.

Example: Within the Occupational Therapy department there are various units like sensory motor lab, developmental disability lab, cognitive perceptual lab, ergonomic lab, assistive and adaptive devices lab etc. Procuring an equipment is the need of the hour at sensory motor lab, so a slightly higher budget can be proposed for the same compared to budget required for other labs.

2. **Capital Budget**

Capital Budget reflects the total expenses of the organization. This budget includes the expenses incurred to improve certain facilities at the department/hiring a new employee for the department etc. This capital budget is a budget planned for 2-5 years and the equipment/facilities should at least have five-year expectancy. The format of capital budget varies from one organization to another.

Example: allocating funds for renovating or expanding therapy facilities to accommodate a growing patient base or to create a more conductive environment.

2. REVENUE, EXPENSE AND OPERATING BUDGET

Revenue and Expense Budget reflects the expected revenues from the payment of services rendered, grants, endowments, special funds etc. organization for a particular year. Other budgets also include personnel budget, employee budget, equipment budget, development budget etc.

FUNDING

Funding refers to the profession of financial resources or capital to support a particular project, initiative, organization activity or conduct research. It involves of the allocation of money to meet specific needs. It can come from various sources including government grants, private donation, investments or other source of financial support and is essential for the successful implementation and continuation of project and activities.

The initial step is to write a proposal which involves developing an idea, aligning it with organizational and funding agency priorities. Challenges which are faced by the occupational therapy practitioner can be turned into opportunities in potential ideas or solutions to these problems are put into a proposal. grant writers should demonstrate clear interest in the idea, backed by knowledge of their organization's expertise and the funding agencies interest. Strategies during the idea development phase include reviewing current research, exploring professional resources, and conducting interviews with field experts. This process, spanning months, culminates in a well-defined proposal.

FUNDING SOURCES

After refining the idea, the next step involves identifying potential funding sources that align with the idea's interests and priorities. This requires a systematic prospect research approach, categorizing potential funders into "yes," "maybe," and "no" based on their alignment with the grant writer's programs. The development of a comprehensive database aids in organizing this information, enabling quick retrieval and efficient tracking of grant cycles. This strategic approach enhances the likelihood of securing funding for the refined idea.

There are two types of funding source categories

1. Public (federal and state agencies)
2. Private (private foundations, professional associations and private business/ industries)

Membership-based tools like Community of Science (COS) and Grant Select are widely used for locating private or public funding sources. COS, a leading information provider, offers a Database of Funded Research with records on opportunities worth over $35 billion. It serves more than 1,600 universities, corporations, and government agencies globally, providing free individual membership for grant seekers. Grant Select, another online database, lists over 12,500 funding opportunities from 5,800 sponsors, allowing keyword searches for targeted notifications. Grant Select requires a membership fee.

After gathering information, grant writers should thoroughly review grant maker announcements, understand proposal components, and contact the project officer or contact person to clarify intent and expectations. Strategies during the fund matching and prospect research phase include requesting or downloading application packets, seeking insights from past grantees or reviewers, and developing a list of questions to address with the grant maker's project officer through a phone call or personal visit.

1. PUBLIC

Public funding sources depends on federal and state agencies. The federal government is the largest training funding. Most federal agencies such as

- National Institutes of Health (NIH)
- National Science Foundation,
- Department of Health and Human Services
- Centers for Disease Control and Prevention (CDC)
- Health Resources and Services Administration
- Department of Education
- Department of Defense.

They offer grant programs aligning with their mission. Tools like Grants.gov, Catalog of Federal Domestic Assistance, Federal Register, and Commerce Business Daily aid in identifying specific funding opportunities. Grant writers can use these resources for targeted prospect research, ensuring a better fit between individual research interests and available funding opportunities.

2. PRIVATE

Private funding includes private foundations and private business or industry. Private foundations in the United States, numbering over 43,000, contribute more than $8 billion annually to research funding. Federal law mandates foundations to give away at least 5 percent of their market-value assets or interest income annually. The Foundation Center (http://foundationcenter.org) and the Council on Foundations (http://www.cof.org/links) offer comprehensive listings of state grant makers, providing electronic lists and print resources. Grant writers can use these tools to enhance their awareness of available funding opportunities within their state or geographic location.

CHAPTER FIVE

QUALITY ASSURANCE

INTRODUCTION

Quality assurance can be defined as "*part of quality management focused on providing confidence that quality requirements will be fulfilled.*" It includes range of activities (including review, evaluation, surveillance, appraisal and monitoring) which collectively comprise the intelligence gathering arm of quality assurance.

- **REVIEW**

It is the process of critical reflection used by clinicians wishing to assess their own (or their peers) performance.

- **AUDIT**

Audit is a part of the quality assurance function. It is important to ensure quality because it is used to compare actual conditions with requirements and to report those results to management.

- **EVALUATION**

Evaluation is one- off assessment of the impact of a service on indices of health.

- **SURVEILLENCE**

It is the routinely repeated evaluation.

- **APPRAISAL**

Appraisal is ad hoc data collection and analysis by management in relation to health care delivery.

- **MONITORING**

It is the ongoing appraisal.

I. **UTILISATION REVIEW**

Utilization review involves "*evaluation of the necessity, appropriateness, and efficiency of the use of healthcare services, procedures, and facilities*" and has become "one of the primary tools utilized by health plans to control over-utilization, reduce costs, and manage care". Utilization reviews take place over the course of patient treatment, including the quest for approval before scheduling a procedure.

Utilisation review occur in three main stages which are:

i. **PROSPECTIVE**

In this stage, a patient seeks approval in preparation for care. For example, a patient schedules elective surgery and the UR process determines the course of treatment including medical history, staff requirements, hospital room use and length of stay, technologies and procedures implemented and corresponding costs.

i. **CONCURRENT**

Reviews take place during care to evaluate medical necessity. This might include deciding to move patients to appropriate units or facilities for high-quality and economical healthcare.

For example, during a therapy session, the occupational therapist takes real-time notes on the client's activities, responses, and progress. This can include observations of fine motor skills, cognitive engagement, and emotional well-being.

iii. RETROSPECTIVE

This review evaluates after-care plans including outpatient therapies. It also serves to review rendered care to determine historic medical necessity.

For example: At the end of a treatment period, the occupational therapist reviews the overall progress and outcomes achieved by the client. Retrospective documentation involves summarizing the entire course of therapy, highlighting milestones, challenges, and the effectiveness of interventions.

II. PROGRAM EVALUATION

Program evaluation and quality assurance helps organizations ensure that they are meeting the right needs of the right people in the best and most efficient way through *the systematic collection, analysis and use of information*. For defining a program, it is important to define the expected outcomes (Valluzzi, 2002), how the program is to be evaluated, and what indicators are to be used.

INDICATORS
USE
MEASURE

1ST SET

To measure the safety and effectiveness of services

rendered to clients

standardized functional measures, rapidity of discharge to a lower level of care, and reduced recidivism

2ND SET

To analyse the revenues and whether the program is on budget and

meeting financial projections.

include objective measures of outcome appropriate for the client population; client satisfaction surveys

Often the people involved in the program want to know:

- if the program is meeting its goals,
- if the goals are appropriate to what the people who use the services want and need
- to the values and mission of the program,
- what resources the program needs and how it is using them,
- if there are other alternatives to meet the goals and
- if there are any unintended consequences of the program.

Program evaluation helps to develop systems to answer these questions and make use the information.

II. QUALITY ASSURANCE MONITORING

Monitoring is essential to ensure that the intended project objective can be achieved within the given time frame following the activities as planned to be carried out by project personnel.

Any intervention effort should attempt to document the process of implementing (process indicators) as well as measuring change (outcome indicators) that might have taken place due to such intervention in a population group. Both process and outcome indicators can and should be measured by quantitative as well as qualitative data.

QUALITY ENHANCEMENT

Quality enhancement refers to systematic efforts and processes aimed at improving the overall quality of services, products, or processes. In occupational therapy it involves continuous assessment, refinement, and optimization of intervention and practices to ensure they meet or exceed established standards. It is crucial because it ensures that intervention and services provided are effective, safe, and client centred.

I. QUALITY ENHANCEMENT PROGRAMS

There are two quality enhancement programs that are popular and are currently used, with evidence-based practice which are:

- Continuous quality improvement
- Six sigma strategic process management

i. CONTINUOUS QUALITY IMPROVEMENT

Continuous Quality Improvement (CQI), developed by W. Edwards Deming, is a management process evaluating the arrangement of people, equipment, and procedures to consistently produce desired results. Products and services result from processes, and quality issues arise when processes go awry. The FOCUS-PDCA model, frequently employed in healthcare, is a nine-step approach within CQI. It aids in identifying and rectifying problem areas, fostering higher quality performance in a timely manner.

1. FIND a process that requires improvement.
2. ORGANIZE a working group that understands what needs to be improved.
3. CLARIFY the issues surrounding the process by asking "who, what, when, and where."
4. UNDERSTAND the factors that are causing inconsistency in performance by asking "why."
5. SELECT a solution-that has been identified to improve the process. This is the step in which errors can be made by hurrying to select an intervention strategy that may not improve the outcomes of the process being examined.
6. PLAN to improve the process being analysed. Brainstorming, diagramming, goal setting, and action planning for data collection are performed.
7. DO identified improvement measures on a small scale while closely monitoring the process.

8. CHECK to assess if the plan for improvement to the process was effectively implemented and to examine the effects of the change vs. what was predicted. If results are less than desired, then a review of FOCUS-PDCA steps is in order. If results are satisfactory and process improvement is noted, then proceed to the last step.
9. ACT to ensure that improvements are maintained and to improve the team performance during the FOCUS-PDCA cycle.

ii. **SIX SIGMA STRATEGIC PROCESS MANAGEMENT**

Six Sigma, originating at Motorola in 1986, initially aimed at improving manufacturing and reducing errors, has expanded into healthcare. Utilizing statistical methods, it targets defect elimination, defined as anything potentially leading to customer dissatisfaction. Leaders undergo extensive training, emphasizing fact-based decision-making. The Six Sigma process follows the DMAIC approach (define, measure, analyse, improve, control), mirroring the CQI-PDCA model.

ii.

www.ingramcontent.com/pod-product-compliance
Lightning Source LLC
LaVergne TN
LVHW021142160826
845679LV00023B/2020

* 9 7 9 8 8 9 2 3 3 2 9 2 7 *